The Solar System

Pluto

Robin Birch

CHELSEA CLUBHOUSE
An Imprint of Chelsea House Publishers
A Haights Cross Communications Company
Philadelphia

This edition first published in 2004 in the United States of America by Chelsea Clubhouse, a division of Chelsea House Publishers and a subsidiary of Haights Cross Communications.

All rights reserved. No part of this publication may be reproduced or transmitted in any form or by any means without the written permission of the publisher.

Chelsea House Publishers
1974 Sproul Road, Suite 400
Broomall, PA 19008-0914

The Chelsea House world wide web address is www.chelseahouse.com

Library of Congress Cataloging-in-Publication Data Applied for.
ISBN 0-7910-7931-7

First published in 2004 by
MACMILLAN EDUCATION AUSTRALIA PTY LTD
627 Chapel Street, South Yarra, Australia, 3141

Associated companies and representatives throughout the world.

Copyright © Robin Birch 2004
Copyright in photographs © individual photographers as credited

Edited by Anna Fern
Text and cover design by Cristina Neri, Canary Design
Illustrations by Melissa Webb
Photo research by Legend Images

Printed in China

Acknowledgements
The author and publisher are grateful to the following for permission to reproduce copyright material:

Cover photograph of Pluto courtesy of Photolibrary.com/SPL.

Art Archive, p. 4 (bottom centre); Photometric/M.Buie—Lowell Observatory/Tom Stack/Auscape, p. 24; TSADO/NASA/Tom Stack/Auscape, p. 28; Australian Picture Library/Corbis, pp. 7, 20; ESA, p. 5; ESA/NASA/Dr. R. Albrecht, p. 21; Calvin J. Hamilton, pp. 9, 29; Walter Myers/www.arcadiastreet.com, pp. 14, 18; NASA/ESA/Alan Stern (Southwest Research Institute), Marc Buie (Lowell Institute), p. 16; NASA/JPL, pp. 15, 17 (top left); NASA/US Geological Survey, p. 17 (top right); Photodisc, p. 27; Photolibrary.com/SPL, pp. 4 (bottom left), 6, 8, 17 (bottom), 19, 22, 25, 26.

Background and border images courtesy of Photodisc, and view of Pluto courtesy of NASA/ESA/Alan Stern (Southwest Research Institute), Marc Buie (Lowell Institute).

While every care has been taken to trace and acknowledge copyright, the publisher tenders their apologies for any accidental infringement where copyright has proved untraceable. Where the attempt has been unsuccessful, the publisher welcomes information that would redress the situation.

Please note
At the time of printing, the Internet addresses appearing in this book were correct. Owing to the dynamic nature of the Internet, however, we cannot guarantee that all these addresses will remain correct.

Contents

Discovering Pluto	4
The Ninth Planet	8
On Pluto	10
Pluto's Moon	20
Exploring Pluto	26
Pluto Fact Summary	30
Glossary	31
Index	32

Glossary words

When you see a word printed in bold, **like this**, you can look up its meaning in the glossary on page 31.

Discovering Pluto

The **planet** Pluto was discovered in 1930. It was the last planet in the solar system to be discovered.

Pluto was discovered by Clyde Tombaugh at a time when **astronomers** were searching for another planet further out than the planets Uranus and Neptune. A powerful **telescope** is needed to see Pluto. Even then, it is small, faint, and difficult to see.

▼ The planet Pluto

◄ The Roman god Pluto

Pluto is the Roman god of the underworld. The planet Pluto was given this name because it is in a place that is very dark and far away, like the underworld. The name "Pluto" was suggested by a schoolgirl in England.

▲ This is the symbol for Pluto.

The word "planet" means "wanderer." Stars always make the same pattern in the sky. Planets slowly change their location in the sky, compared to the stars around them. This is why planets were called "wanderers."

▲ An artist's impression of a Pluto-like body.

Search for New Planets

The planet Neptune was discovered in 1846. After that, astronomers studied the movements of Uranus and Neptune and decided they did not make sense. They thought there must be one or more undiscovered planets with **gravity** strong enough to pull on Uranus and Neptune, affecting their movements.

Many astronomers began searching for more planets. They worked out where in the sky they thought the planets should be by studying the movement and **mass** of known planets and comets. Hundreds of photographs of the sky were taken and looked at very carefully, for something that had not been seen before.

Planet X

An astronomer called Percival Lowell began searching for just one planet which he called "Planet X." Lowell worked out where he thought he would find the planet and studied hundreds of photographs of the sky. He died in 1916, without finding Planet X.

A young astronomer called Clyde Tombaugh was hired in April 1929 to search for Planet X. He looked in the parts of the sky where Lowell had thought Planet X would be. After taking thousands of photographs of millions of **stars**, Tombaugh found a new planet in February 1930. The new planet was called Pluto.

> Percival Lowell was an American astronomer, born in 1855. He founded the Lowell Observatory, in Arizona. Lowell thought that the lines he saw on Mars were canals.

◀ Percival Lowell

Clyde Tombaugh was an American astronomer, born in 1906. He found Pluto because he searched his photographs very thoroughly, but it was not the planet he was looking for.

◀ Clyde Tombaugh

Astronomers thought that Pluto was not heavy enough to affect the movements of Uranus and Neptune and decided that Pluto was not Planet X. Clyde Tombaugh kept searching for Planet X for another 13 years, looking at 90 million photographs of most of the sky. He decided that there could not be a Planet X, or he would have found it.

When astronomers eventually worked out more accurate masses for Uranus and Neptune, the movements of these planets made more sense. Astronomers decided there was no other planet, and the search for Planet X came to an end.

The Ninth Planet

The small, icy planet Pluto is part of the solar system, which consists mainly of the Sun and nine planets. The planets **revolve** around the Sun. Pluto is the ninth and farthest planet from the Sun.

The solar system also has comets and asteroids moving around in it. Comets are large balls of rock, ice, **gas**, and dust which **orbit** the Sun. Comets start their orbit far away from the Sun. They travel in close to the Sun, go around it, and then travel out again. When they come close to the Sun, comets grow a tail.

Asteroids are rocks. There are millions of asteroids in the solar system. They can be small or large. The largest asteroid, named Ceres, is about 584 miles (940 kilometers) across. Most asteroids orbit the Sun in a path called the asteroid belt, between the orbits of Mars and Jupiter.

▶ The solar system

The solar system is about 4,600 million years old.

The planets in the solar system are made of rock, ice, gas, and liquid. Mercury, Venus, Earth, and Mars are made of rock. Pluto is probably made of rock and ice. These are the smallest planets.

Jupiter, Saturn, Uranus, and Neptune are made mainly of gas and liquid. They are the largest planets. They are often called the gas giants, because they have no solid ground to land on.

Planets, comets, and asteroids are lit up by light from the Sun. They do not make their own light the way stars do.

▶ The planets, from smallest to largest, are: Pluto, Mercury, Mars, Venus, Earth, Neptune, Uranus, Saturn, and Jupiter.

Planet	Average distance from Sun	
Mercury	35,960,000 miles	(57,910,000 kilometers)
Venus	67,190,000 miles	(108,200,000 kilometers)
Earth	92,900,000 miles	(149,600,000 kilometers)
Mars	141,550,000 miles	(227,940,000 kilometers)
Jupiter	483,340,000 miles	(778,330,000 kilometers)
Saturn	887,660,000 miles	(1,429,400,000 kilometers)
Uranus	1,782,880,000 miles	(2,870,990,000 kilometers)
Neptune	2,796,000,000 miles	(4,504,000,000 kilometers)
Pluto	3,672,300,000 miles	(5,913,520,000 kilometers)

The name "solar system" comes from the word "Solaris." This is the official name for the Sun. The Sun is a star.

On Pluto

As it travels around the Sun, the small, icy planet Pluto spins on its **axis**.

Rotation and Revolution

Pluto **rotates** on its axis once every 6.39 Earth days. It rotates backwards, compared to most other planets.

Pluto spins almost on its side, compared to other planets. This means that when a **pole** is pointing towards the Sun, that pole has one long day, which lasts for many Earth years. When a pole is pointing away from the Sun, that pole has one long night. When the Sun is shining on the **equator**, a day and a night on Pluto take about six and a half days of Earth time.

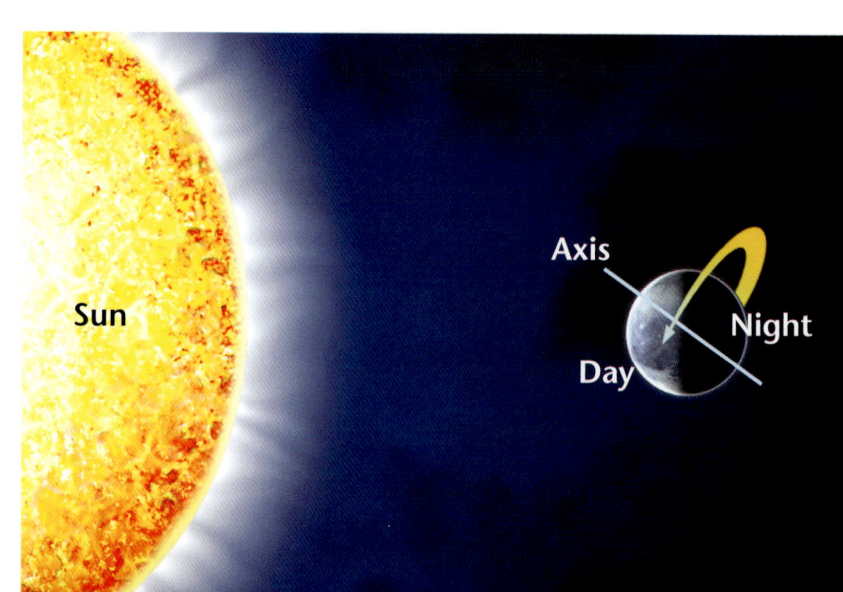

▶ Pluto rotates on its axis as it revolves around the Sun.

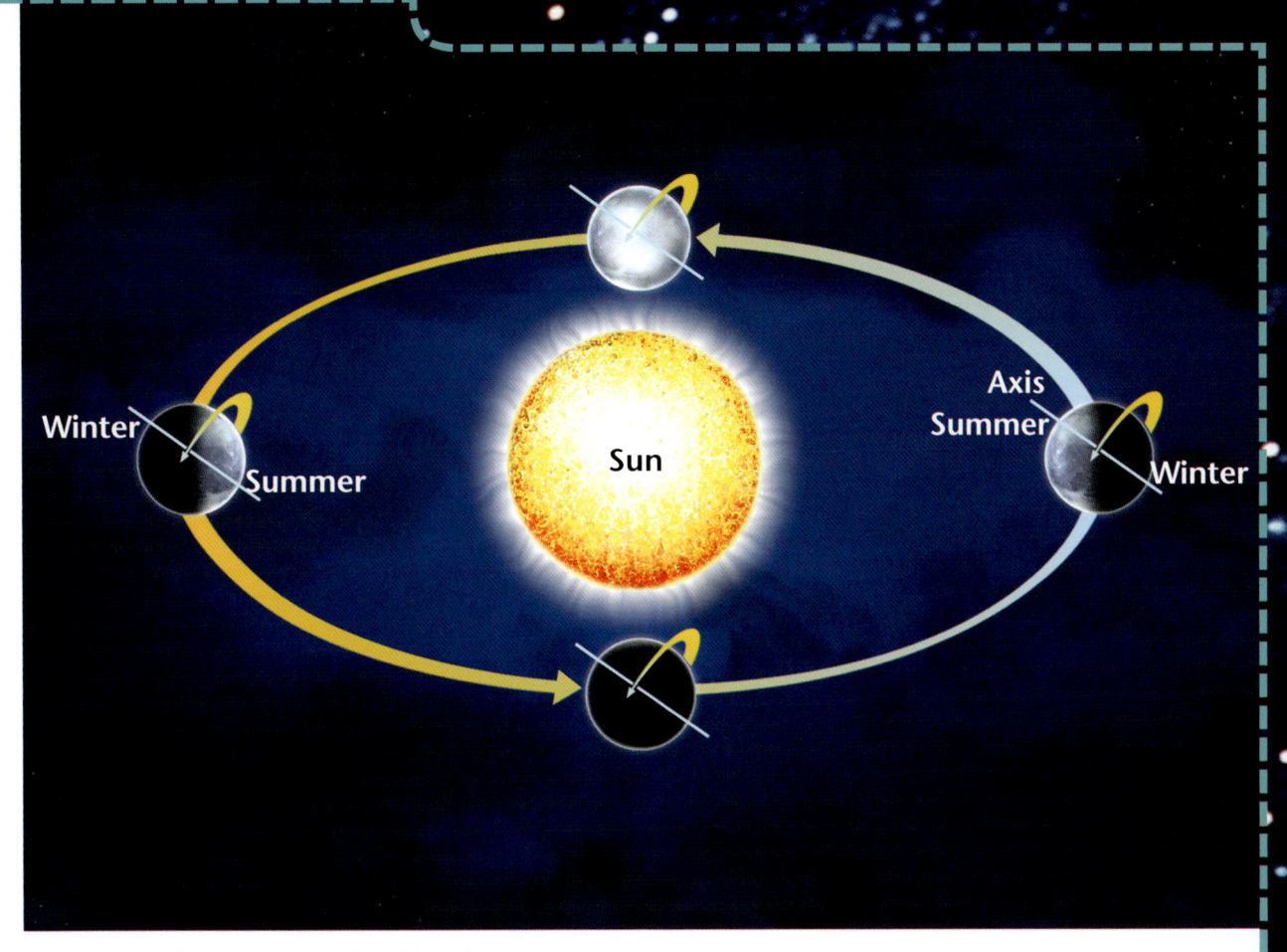

▲ The seasons in Pluto's year

Pluto orbits the Sun once every 247.7 Earth years, which is the length of a year on Pluto. The Sun's strong gravity keeps Pluto revolving around it.

Seasons

Pluto has seasons as it travels around the Sun. The seasons are very long, because Pluto spins lying almost on its side. When the poles face the Sun, they have very long summers. When the poles face away from the Sun, they have very long winters. When Pluto was discovered in 1930, the bright south pole area was facing Earth, and the Sun. By 1973, people on Earth got a view of the equator area.

Orbit

Pluto revolves around the Sun in an elliptical, or oval-shaped orbit. When Pluto is closest to the Sun, it is 2,748 million miles (4,425 million kilometers) from the Sun. When Pluto is farthest from the Sun, it is 4,803 million miles (7,735 million kilometers) from the Sun. Pluto was at its closest point to the Sun in 1989. It will not be this close to the Sun again until the year 2236. When Pluto came closer to the Sun, it was also closer to Earth, so it was a good time to study Pluto.

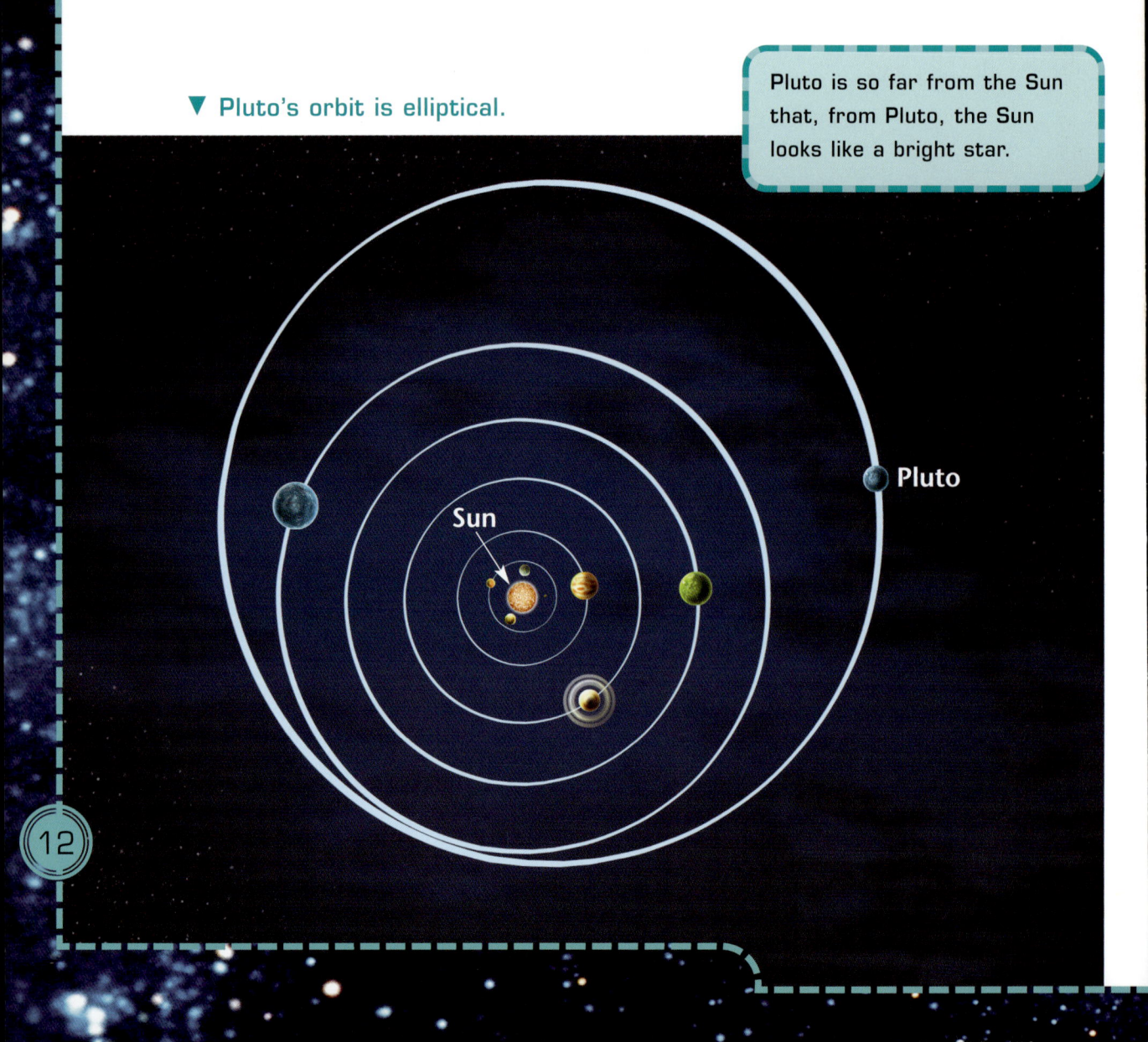

▼ Pluto's orbit is elliptical.

Pluto is so far from the Sun that, from Pluto, the Sun looks like a bright star.

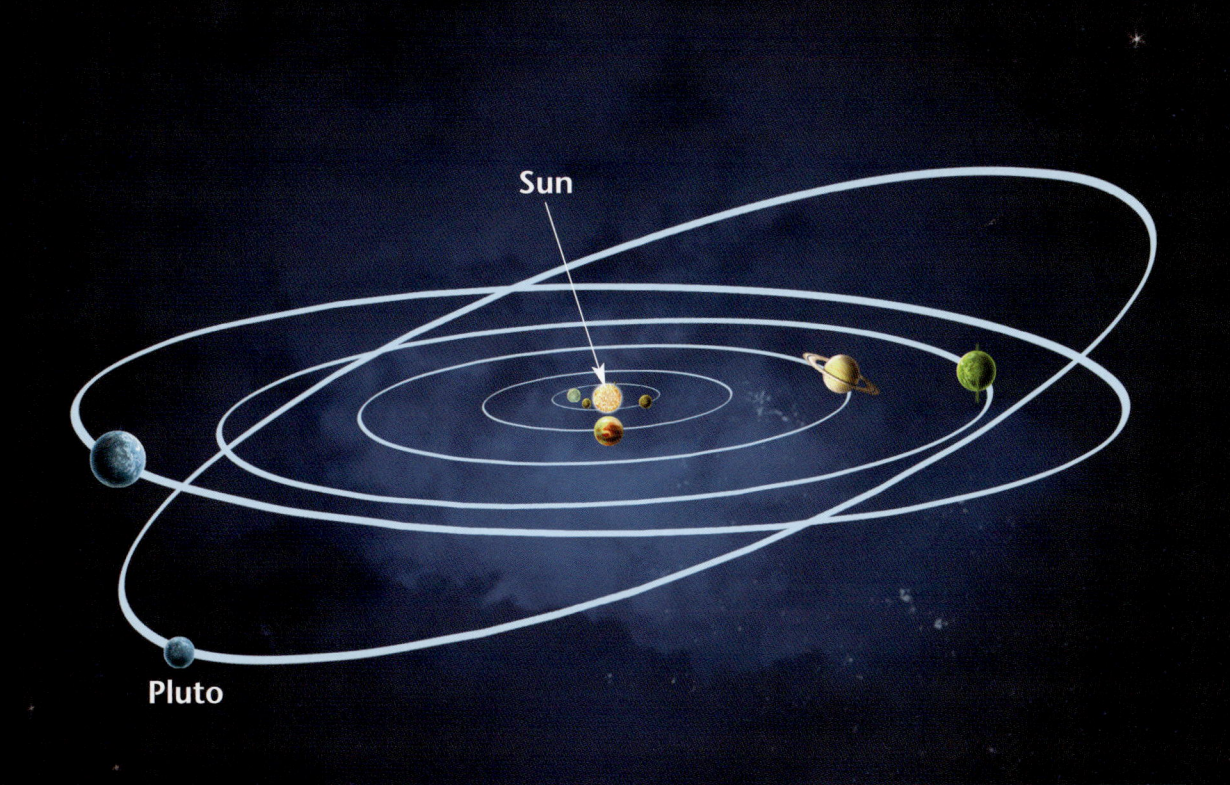

▲ Pluto's orbit is tilted.

Neptune and Pluto will never collide with each other. This is because if they were the same distance from the Sun at the same time, one would be above the other.

When Pluto is closest to the Sun, it is closer to the Sun than the planet Neptune. Pluto was closer to the Sun than Neptune from January 1979 to February 1999.

All the other planets orbit the Sun more or less as though they are on a flat surface. We say that they orbit the Sun in the same **plane**. However, Pluto's orbit is sloping, or tilted, compared to the orbits of other planets. For part of its year Pluto is below the other planets, and for the rest of its year it is above the other planets.

Size and Structure

Pluto is the smallest planet. It is smaller than seven of the **moons** in the solar system, including Earth's Moon. Pluto is two-thirds the **diameter** of Earth's Moon. Pluto is too small and too far away to be measured exactly, but its diameter is estimated to be around 1,418 miles (2,284 kilometers).

▼ Compare the size of Pluto with Earth, Earth's Moon, and Mercury.

Earth

Pluto

Mercury

Earth's Moon

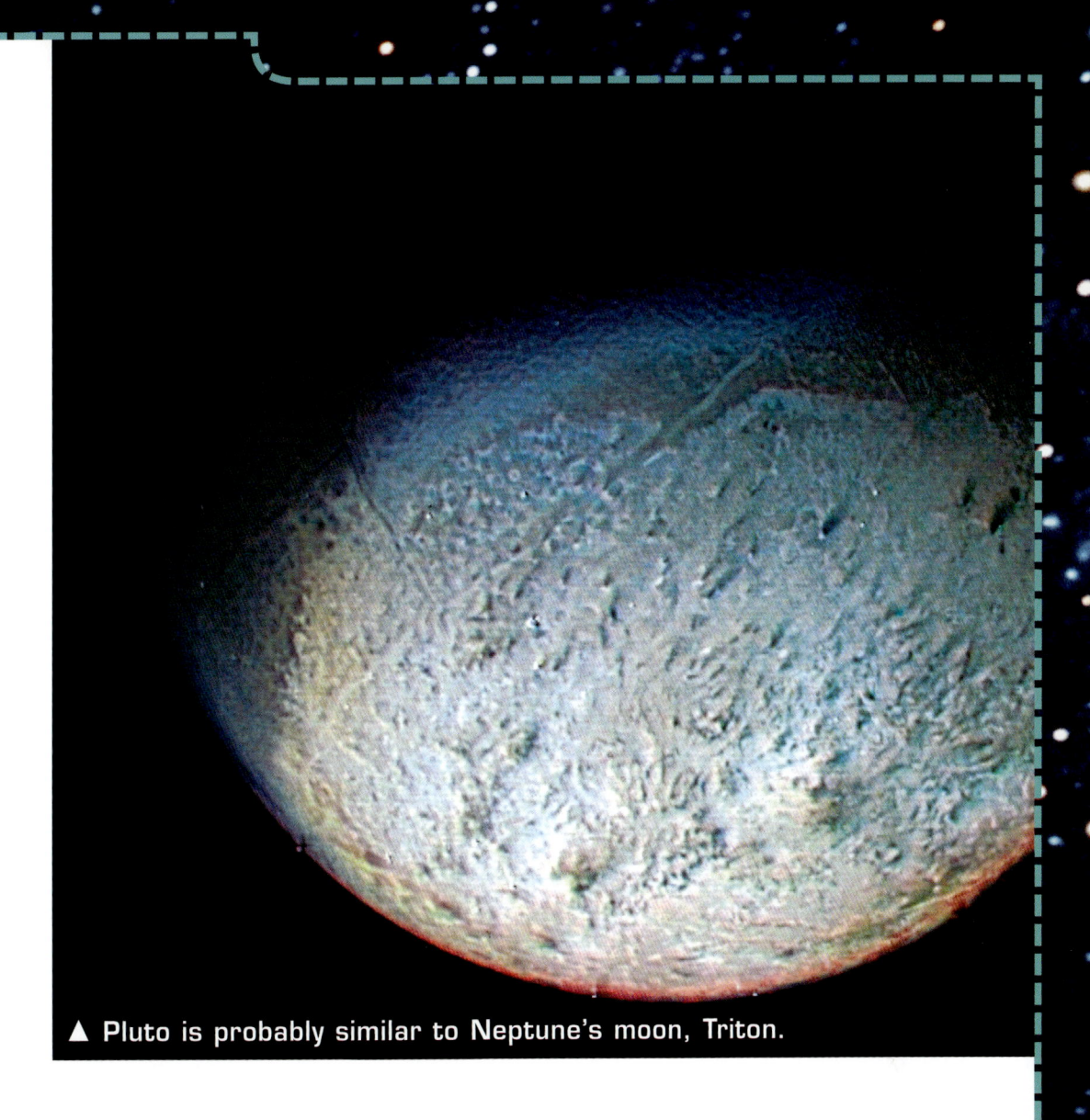

▲ Pluto is probably similar to Neptune's moon, Triton.

   Pluto is probably made of 70 percent rock and 30 percent frozen water. It probably has ices on its surface, made mainly of the substance nitrogen. Pluto probably has very small amounts of methane, ethane, and carbon monoxide on the surface, as well. These ices form a shiny layer on the outside of Pluto.
   Pluto may have a rocky **core** at the center, which is surrounded by frozen water. Pluto probably has a very similar make-up to Neptune's moon Triton.

Light and Dark Areas

Pluto has bright caps at the north and south poles, and dark features around the equator area. These are shown in photographs taken by the *Hubble Space Telescope*. The dark areas may be features such as large **basins** or **craters** made by asteroids hitting Pluto. However, the dark and light areas may be frosts which move about on the surface. Pluto has more difference between its light and dark areas than any other body in the solar system, except for Iapetus, one of Saturn's moons.

The temperature on Pluto varies between about –390 and –345 degrees Fahrenheit (–235 and –210 degrees Celsius). The warmer parts are the parts that appear darker.

▼ These pictures, taken by the *Hubble Space Telescope*, show opposite sides of Pluto.

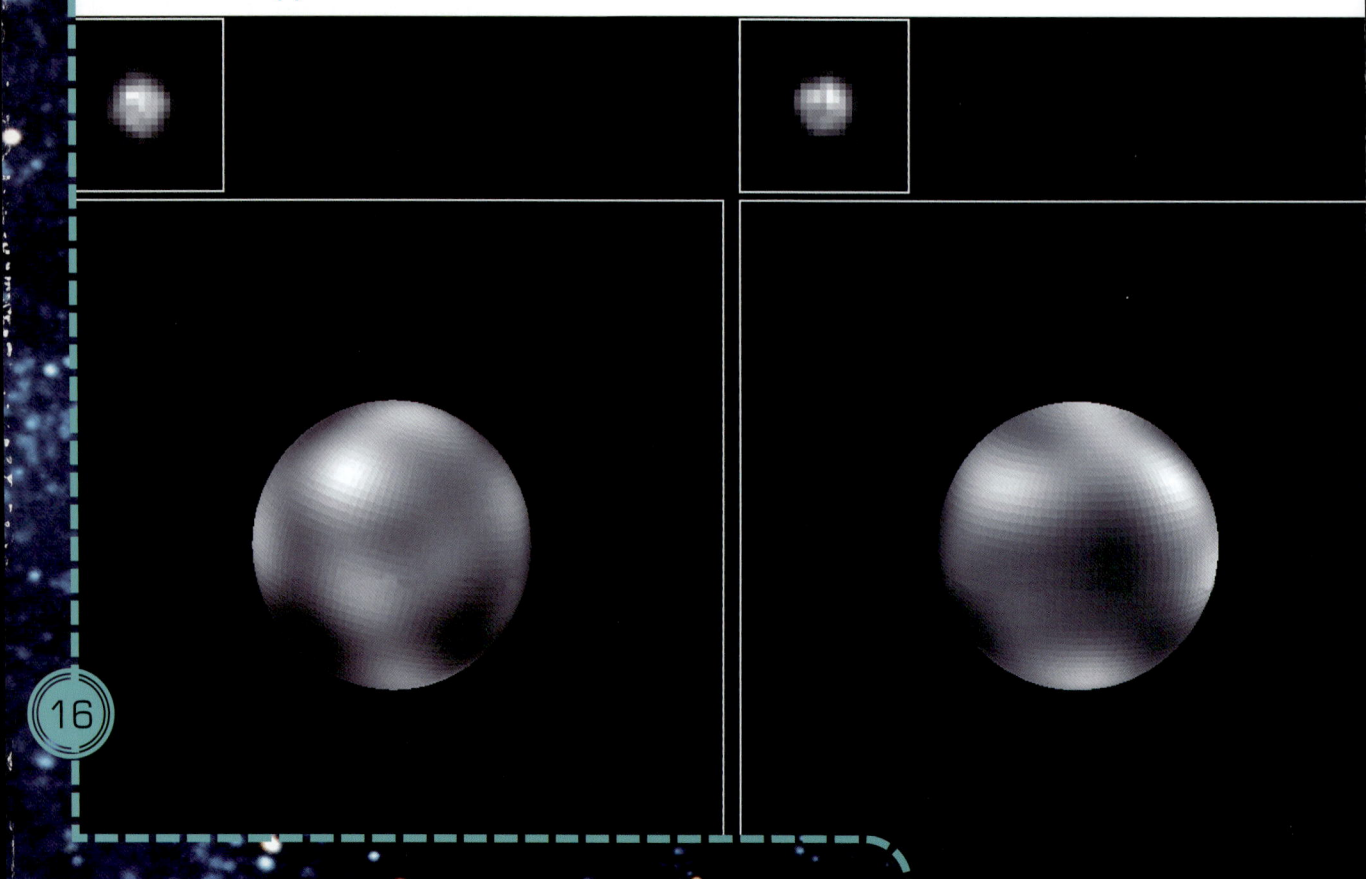

▲ An asteroid (pictured above), a comet (to the right), and an ice dwarf (bottom)

Is Pluto Really a Planet?

Some people think Pluto should be called an asteroid, a comet, or an **ice dwarf**, rather than a planet. This is because Pluto is so small, so far away, and so cold and icy, and because it has an unusually shaped orbit. There are many other bodies similar to Pluto in the outer solar system. Some say that if Pluto was discovered today, no one would bother calling it a planet.

Atmosphere

Not much is known about Pluto's **atmosphere**, but it probably consists mainly of the substance nitrogen. The atmosphere may also have smaller amounts of carbon monoxide and methane in it.

Pluto's orbit takes it closer to the Sun and then farther away from the Sun. When Pluto comes closer to the Sun, it becomes warmer. Then the substances on the surface **evaporate**, making an atmosphere. When Pluto moves far away from the Sun, it becomes colder. Then the substances in the atmosphere freeze and fall down to the surface.

▼ An artist's impression of Pluto when it is farther from the Sun

▲ An artist's impression of Pluto when it is closer to the Sun

▲ Artist's impression of Pluto (in the foreground) and its moon Charon. Pluto's atmosphere can be seen as a haze on the planet's surface.

   Pluto's atmosphere is very light and thin. However, it reaches higher up above the ground than Earth's atmosphere does. This is because Pluto has a much weaker gravity than Earth. When Pluto has an atmosphere, some of it probably even escapes into space. Some of it may reach Pluto's moon, Charon.
   Pluto's atmosphere is so thin that the sky would be black on Pluto and the stars would not twinkle. There would be no sound, because sound is carried by substances, such as air.

Pluto's Moon

Pluto has one moon, called Charon. Charon was discovered in 1978, by an American naval astronomer, Jim Christy. Christy was studying photographs of Pluto very closely to learn more about Pluto's position and orbit. He found a bulge on one side of Pluto, which turned out to be a moon.

In Roman myths, Charon was the ferryman who rowed souls across the River Styx to the underworld, where the god Pluto ruled.

◀ Charon the ferryman

▲ This photo of Pluto and Charon was taken by the *Hubble Space Telescope*.

   Charon and Pluto are so close together that they blur together in most photographs. This is why it took so long to discover Charon. Because Charon and Pluto appeared blurred together, astronomers had thought that Pluto was larger than it is. Better photographs show Charon and Pluto as separate bodies. The *Hubble Space Telescope*'s ability to take a picture of Charon and Pluto is similar to taking a picture of a baseball 25 miles (40 kilometers) away.
   After Charon was discovered, astronomers could work out the mass of Pluto more accurately than before.

Charon's Rotation and Revolution

Charon orbits Pluto in 6.39 Earth days. This is the same time Pluto takes to rotate once on its axis. This causes Charon to be always in the same place above Pluto. So, if we could stand on Pluto, Charon would always be in the same place in the sky. It would not rise and set like other moons do.

The same sides of Pluto and Charon always face each other. So, if we were standing on Pluto, Charon would always have the same pattern on it. This is the same as the way we see Earth's Moon, with the same side always facing us.

▼ An artist's impression of how Charon looks from Pluto. The bright star on the right is the Sun.

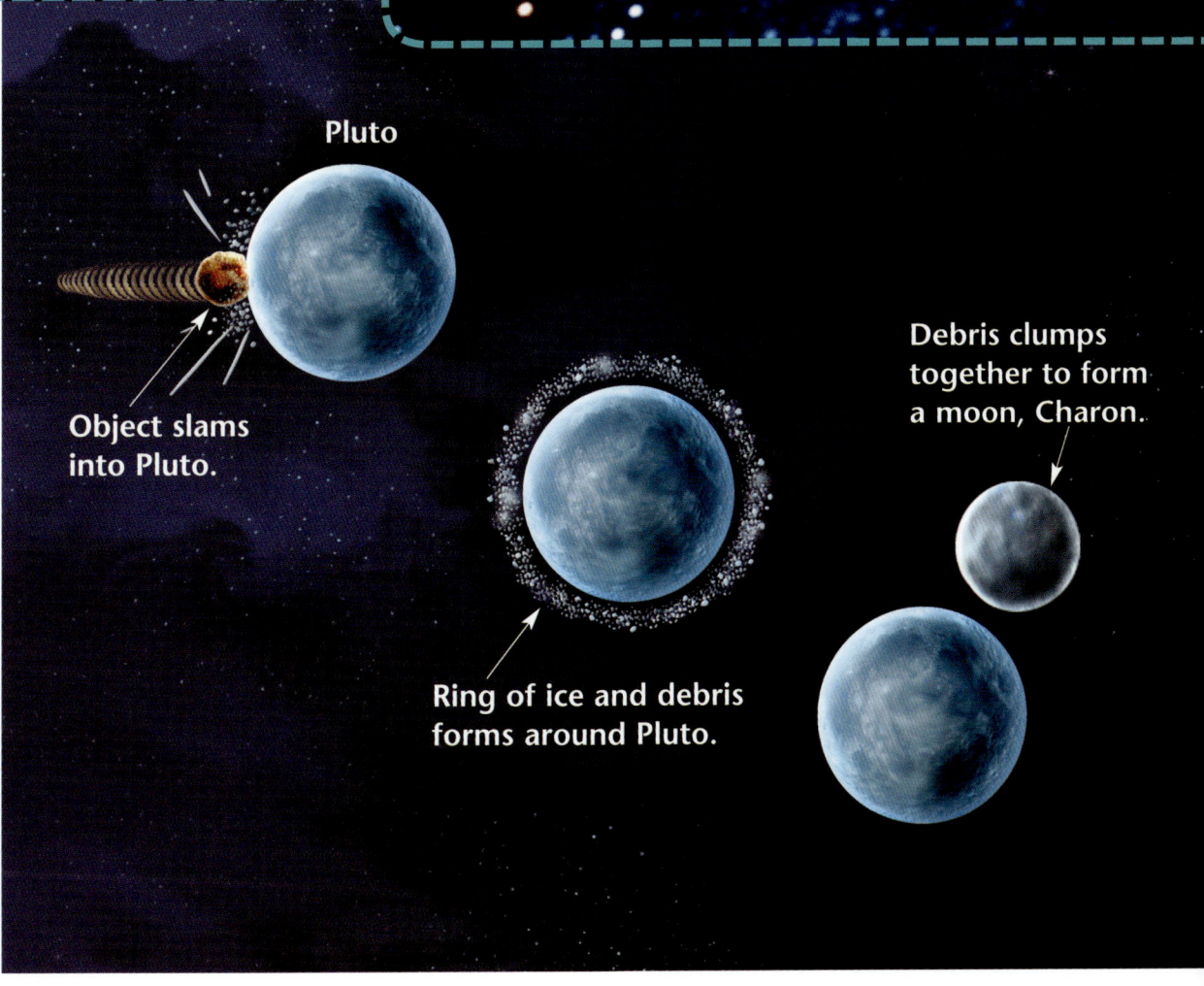

▲ The formation of Charon

Charon and Pluto are only 12,200 miles (19,640 kilometers) apart. This is closer than Earth's Moon is to Earth.

Charon is about half the diameter of Pluto. This means that Charon is big for a moon, compared to Pluto. For this reason, many astronomers say that Charon and Pluto are a double planet.

Charon may have formed after Pluto had a huge collision with another body. The icy and rocky substances thrown up could have reformed to make Pluto and Charon as they are today. This is probably how Earth's Moon was formed.

Charon's Size and Structure

Charon is 728 miles (1,172 kilometers) in diameter and is lightweight for its size. This means that Charon must be made mostly of frozen water and probably a small amount of rock. Charon and Pluto are not made of the same amounts of rock and ice. This means that they could not have formed together.

The surface of Charon is a bluer color than the surface of Pluto. This means that Charon's surface has different substances on it from Pluto's surface. Charon's surface has light and dark patches on it and appears to be covered with water ice. It probably has no atmosphere.

▼ Charon and Pluto

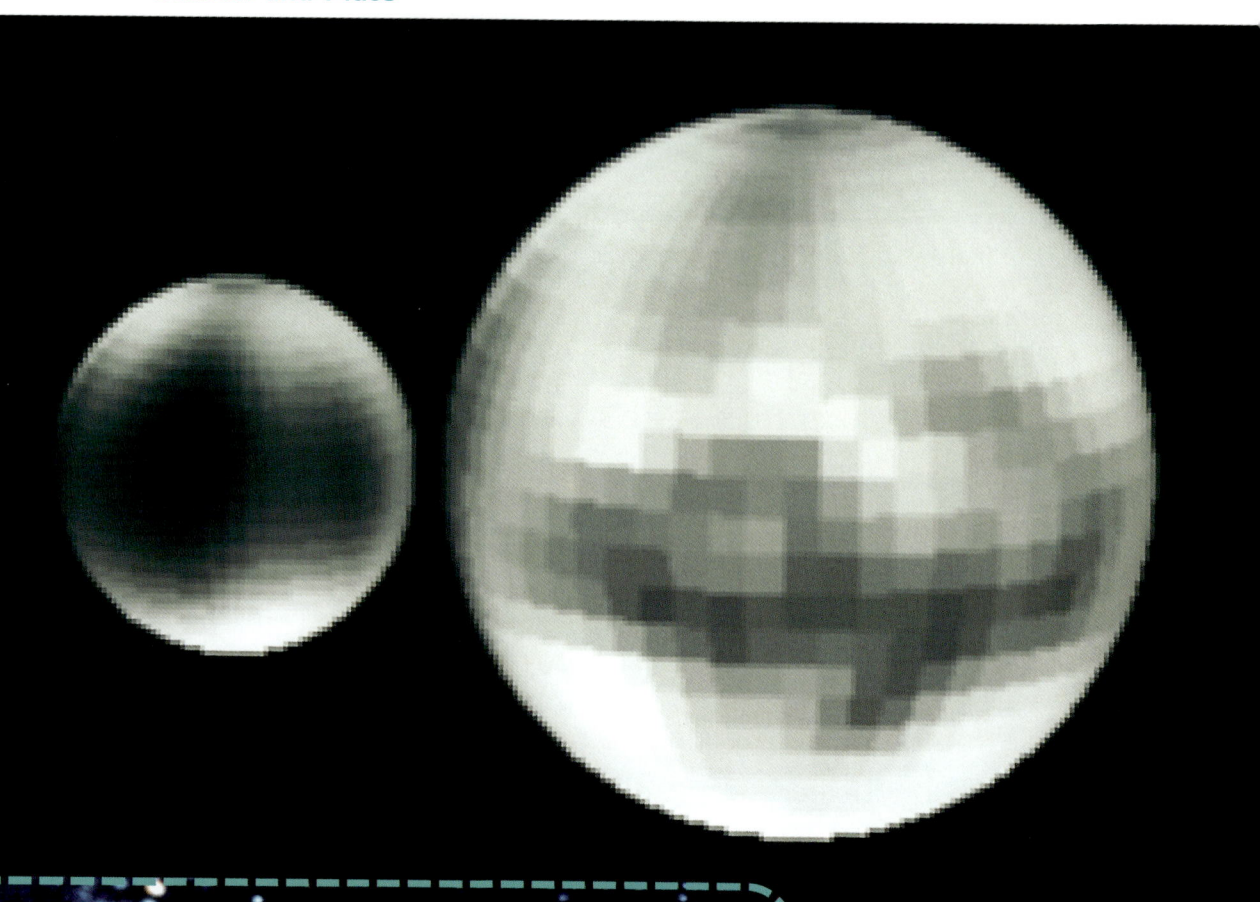

▲ Some Kuiper Belt Objects

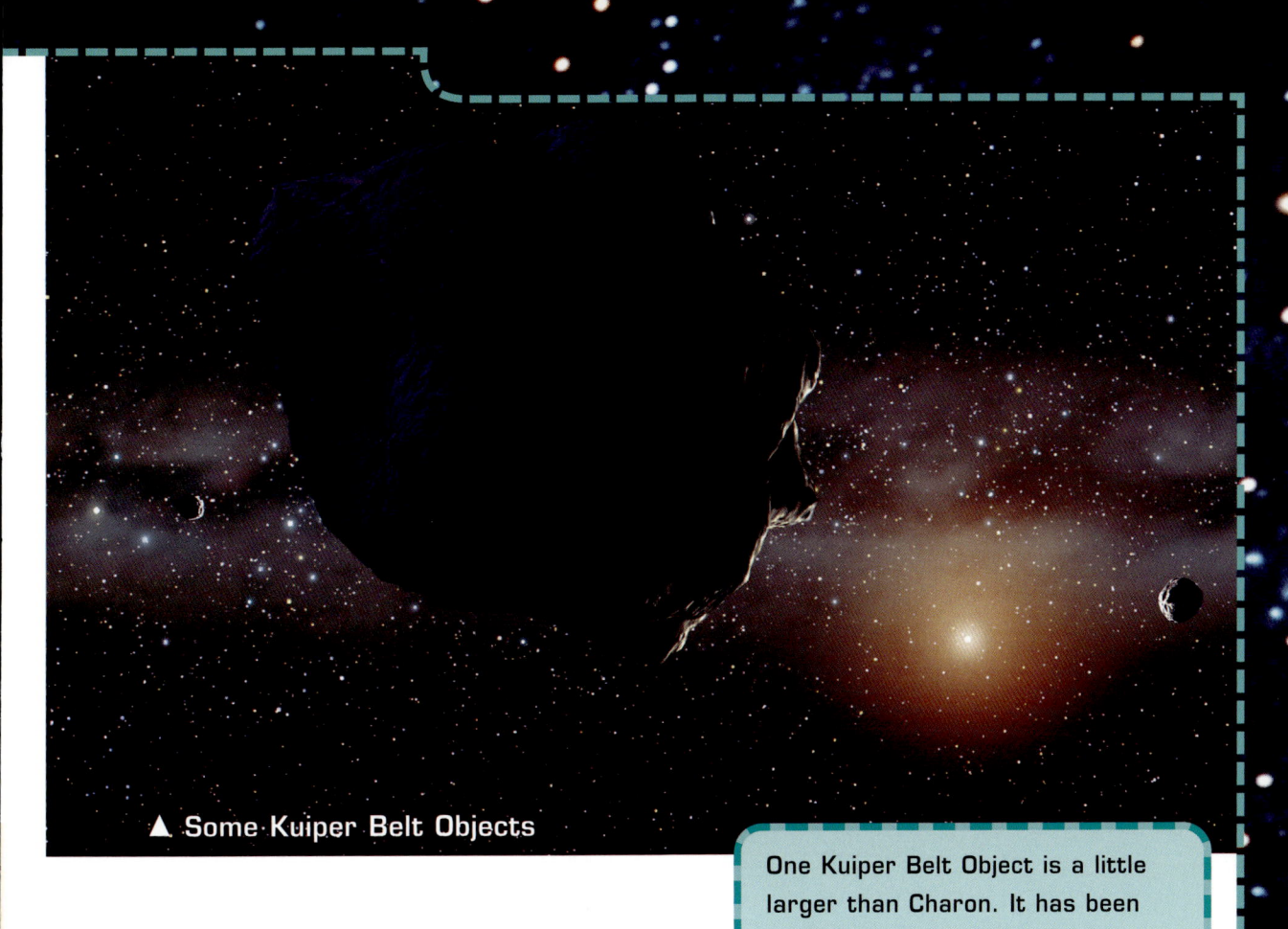

Ice Dwarves

One Kuiper Belt Object is a little larger than Charon. It has been named Quaoar by the astronomers who discovered it.

In the solar system there are many thousands of small, icy bodies further out than Neptune's orbit. They are known as "ice dwarves," or "Kuiper Belt Objects." Thousands of them have diameters greater than 60 miles (100 kilometers). Astronomers think that many comets are ice dwarves that have come from this area.

Pluto and Charon are ice dwarves from the Kuiper Belt. Neptune's moons Triton and Nereid were also probably Kuiper Belt Objects that were trapped by Neptune's gravity. Pluto is the largest known ice dwarf. Many astronomers think that Pluto should be called a Kuiper Belt Object, rather than a planet.

Exploring Pluto

In 1930, Pluto was discovered by the astronomer Clyde Tombaugh, who took photographs of the sky using a camera attached to a telescope. He looked very carefully to see if there was a tiny dot that changed positions between photographs. Tombaugh used a blink microscope. This machine switched quickly between two photographs, so they could be compared quickly and easily.

Today's telescopes show Pluto to be a small, white dot. Pluto is so small that Earth's atmosphere stops any details from being seen.

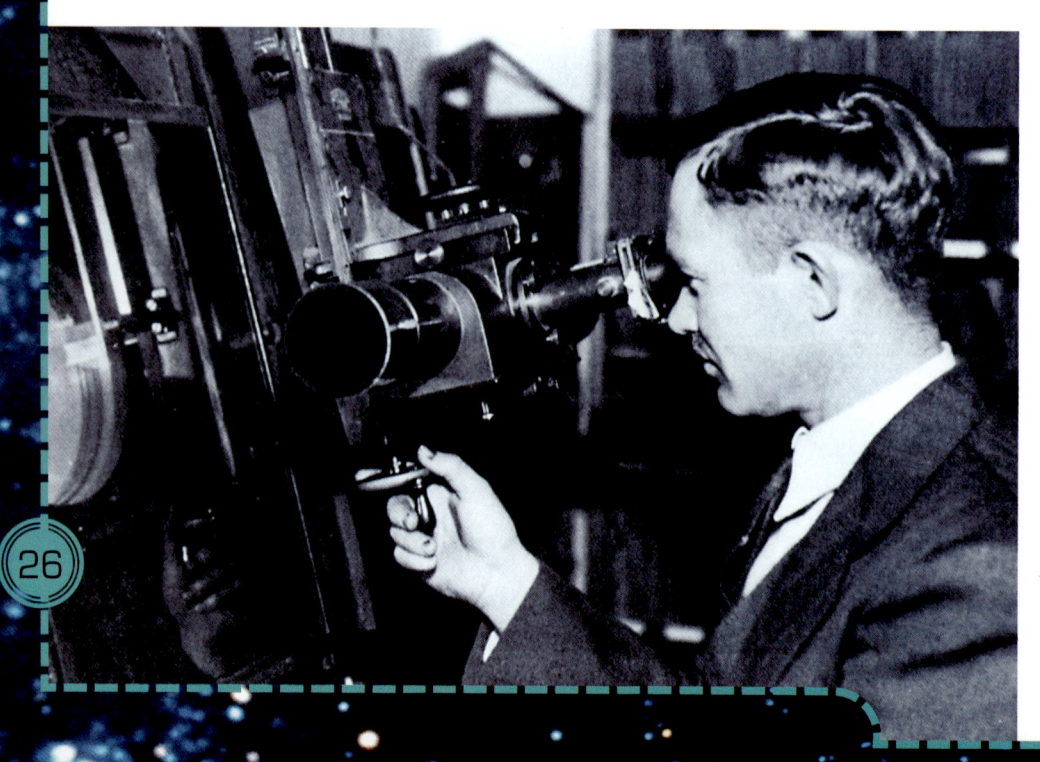

◀ Clyde Tombaugh using a blink microscope

▲ The *Hubble Space Telescope* above Earth

Hubble Space Telescope

The *Hubble Space Telescope (HST)* takes the best pictures of Pluto and Charon today. This telescope orbits Earth above the atmosphere, so the atmosphere does not interfere with the pictures the telescope takes.

The *HST* was launched into space in 1990 on board the space shuttle *Discovery*. When *Discovery* reached space, the *HST* was released to orbit Earth on its own. The *HST* has various cameras and other instruments which record different types of information. They are used to study planets, stars, **galaxies**, **nebulae**, and other objects in space.

Future Exploration

There is a plan to send a **space probe** to visit Pluto, Charon, and the Kuiper Belt. The mission is called *New Horizons*.

The *New Horizons* space probe would be launched in 2006. It would fly past Pluto and Charon in 2015 and would reach the Kuiper Belt by 2026. The *New Horizons* probe will gather information about the bodies it visits. It will study the make-up, surfaces, rocks, and atmospheres of these bodies.

▼ An artist's impression of a space probe visiting Pluto

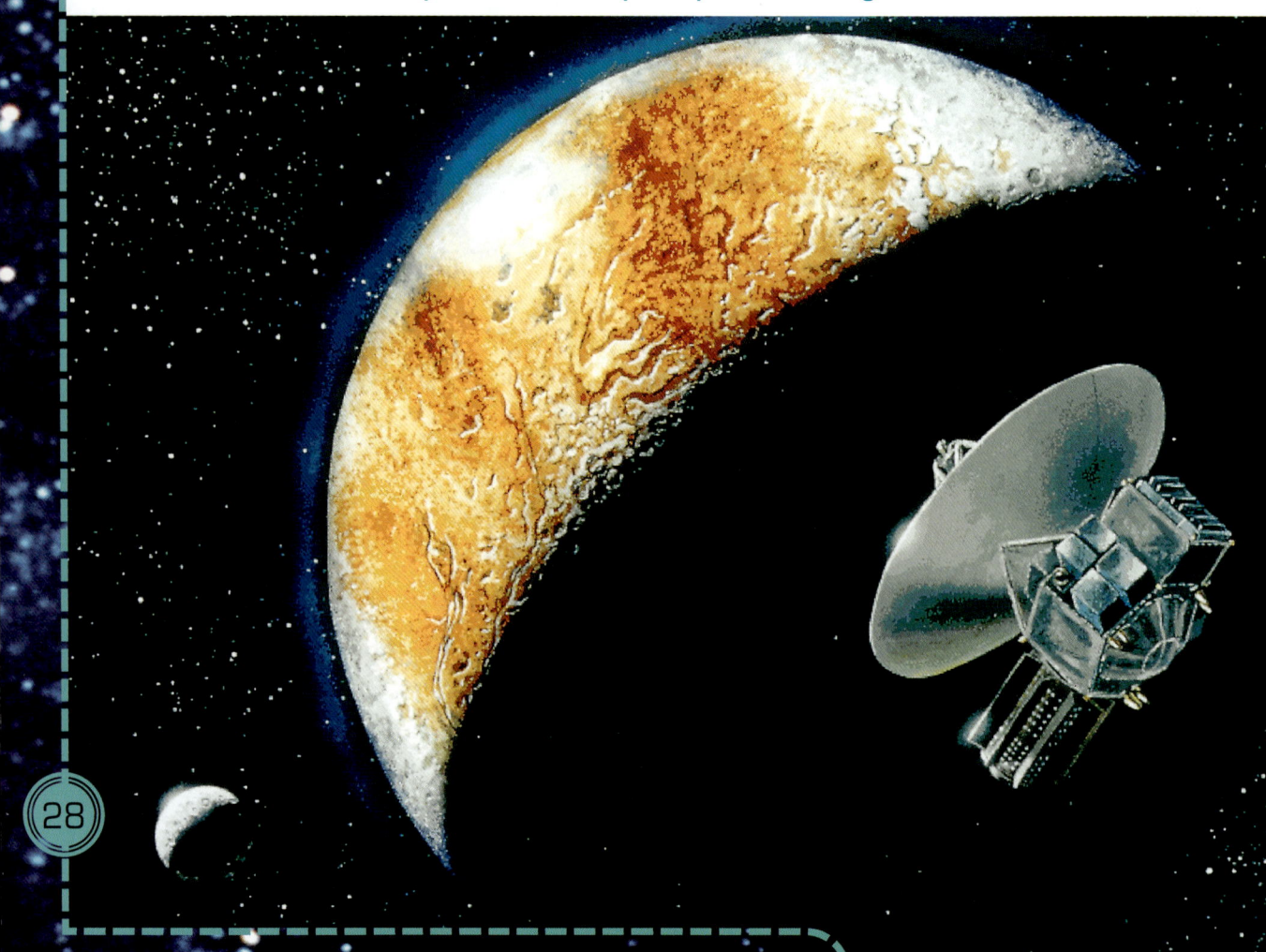

▲ An artist's impression of Pluto's surface

Questions about Pluto

Astronomers are unsure of even the most basic information about Pluto and Charon. They are not even certain of their size, mass, or **density**. One day, astronomers hope to find out the answers to questions such as these:

- What are the dark areas on Pluto?
- Do the surfaces of Pluto and Charon have features such as mountains, valleys, and craters?
- Is there any movement on the surfaces of Pluto and Charon, such as cracks forming in the surface, or icy **volcanoes**?
- What changes happen on Pluto and Charon in the seasons, as Pluto goes through its long year?

Pluto Fact Summary

Distance from Sun (average)	3,672,300,000 miles (5,913,520,000 kilometers)
Diameter (at equator)	1,418 miles (2,284 kilometers)
Mass	0.002 times Earth's mass
Density	1.1 times the density of water
Gravity	0.06 times Earth's gravity
Temperature (surface)	−380 degrees Fahrenheit (−230 degrees Celsius)
Rotation on axis	6.39 Earth days
Revolution	247.7 Earth years
Number of moons	1

Web Sites

www.christinelavin.com/planetx.html
Planet X—a song about the discovery of Pluto

www.nineplanets.org/
The nine planets—a tour of the solar system

www.enchantedlearning.com
Enchanted Learning web site—click on "Astronomy"

stardate.org
Stargazing with the University of Texas McDonald Observatory

pds.jpl.nasa.gov/planets/welcome.htm
Images from NASA's planetary exploration program

Glossary

astronomers people who study stars, planets, and other bodies in space

atmosphere a layer of gas around a large body in space

axis an imaginary line through the middle of an object, from top to bottom

basins very large, bowl-shaped holes

core the inside, or middle part of a planet

craters bowl-shaped holes in the ground

density a measure of how heavy something is for its size

diameter the distance across

equator an imaginary line around the middle of a globe

evaporate change from a liquid into a gas

galaxies huge groups of many millions of stars (the solar system is in the Milky Way galaxy)

gas a substance in which the particles are far apart, so they are not solid or liquid

gravity a force which pulls one body towards another body

ice dwarf an icy body in the outer solar system

mass a measure of how much substance is in something

moons natural bodies which circle around planets

nebulae clouds of gas and dust in space

orbit *noun* the path a body takes when it moves around another body *verb* to travel on a path around another body in space

plane an imaginary flat surface

planet a large body which circles the Sun

pole the top or bottom of a globe

revolve travel around another body

rotates spins

space probe a spacecraft which does not carry people

stars huge balls of glowing gas in space

telescope an instrument for making far away objects look bigger and more detailed

volcanoes holes in the ground through which lava flows

Index

A
asteroids 8, 9, 16, 17
astronomers 4–7, 20–21, 23, 25, 26, 31
atmosphere 18–19, 24, 31

B
basins 16, 31
blink microscope 26

C
carbon monoxide 15, 18
Charon 19, 20–24, 25, 27, 28, 29
Christy, Jim 20
comets 5, 8, 9, 17, 25
core (Pluto) 15, 31
craters 16, 29, 31

D
day (Pluto) 10

E
Earth 11, 14, 19, 26
equator (Pluto) 10, 11, 16, 31
ethane 15

F
frosts 16

G
gravity 5, 11, 19, 25, 30, 31

H
Hubble Space Telescope 16, 21, 27

I
ice 15, 24
ice dwarves 17, 25, 31

K
Kuiper Belt Objects 25

L
Lowell, Percival 6

M
Mercury 14
methane 15, 18
Moon (Earth's) 14, 22, 23
moons 14, 16, 19, 20–24, 25, 30, 31
myths 4, 20

N
Neptune 5, 7, 13, 25
New Horizons 28
night (Pluto) 10
nitrogen 15, 18

O
observing Pluto 4–7, 11, 12, 14, 16, 20–21, 26–8
orbit (Pluto) 10–13, 17, 18, 30, 31

P
Planet X 6–7
planets 4–9, 13, 17, 25, 31
Pluto (Roman god) 4, 20
poles (Pluto) 10, 11, 16, 31

R
revolution (Pluto) 10–11, 30, 31
rotation (Pluto) 10–11, 22, 30, 31

S
seasons 11, 18, 29
size (Pluto) 14, 21, 29, 30
solar system 8–9
space probes 28, 31
stars 5, 9, 19, 31
structure (Pluto) 14–15, 29
Sun 8–9, 10, 11, 12, 13, 18, 30
surface (Charon) 24, 29
surface (Pluto) 15, 16, 29

T
temperature 16, 18, 30
Tombaugh, Clyde 4, 6–7, 26

U
Uranus 5, 7

W
water 15, 24

Y
year (Pluto) 11, 13, 29